SPEAK WITH
POWER, PASSION AND PIZZAZZ!

222 Dynamite Tips to
Dazzle Your Audience

Brent:

kNow Risks. kNow Rewards.

Dr. Prasad Kodukula, PMP
Susan Meyer-Miller

Mav. 8. 2012

HATS
OFF

Speak with Power, Passion and Pizzazz!
222 Dynamite Tips to Dazzle Your Audience

Published by Hats Off Books™
610 East Delano Street, Suite 104
Tucson, Arizona 85705, U.S.A.
www.hatsoffbooks.com

International Standard Book Number: 1-58736-256-2
Library of Congress Control Number: 2003098083

CONTENTS

"I touch the future; I teach."

—*Anonymous*

PREFACE

For most of us, speaking before an audience is not an option; our job requires it. Whether you are:

- a person with a job that involves making frequent sales presentations to your customers

- a manager often talking to your team on how to stay motivated and increase productivity

- a business executive taking a new corporate initiative on the road to rally support from your "troops"

- a project manager meeting regularly with your project sponsor or client to present progress results

- a scientist presenting your research results to your peers at a convention

- a professional speaker or trainer making your living through formal speaking

or whatever your job may be, you are probably finding yourself standing in front of an audience making presentations at an ever-increasing rate. If you are like most people, we suspect that it is something you would rather not do.

According to a February 19–21, 2002 Gallup Poll survey of 1,016 American adults, given a list of things that people fear most, public speaking came in second only to snakes. With the help of the experience we have acquired over the last 20 years of our professional careers, we would like to transform public speaking into an activity that people enjoy rather than fear. As professional speakers and trainers, we have addressed more than a quarter million people in 15 countries on every populated continent throughout the world. Furthermore, we have coached many business professionals, as well as professional speakers and trainers, to greatly improve their speaking abilities. In this book we wanted to share some of our experiences, and show you how you can most effectively communicate your message and dazzle your audience.

There are probably more than one hundred books available on public speaking. Why another book? In today's world, we, as speakers, are dealing with an entirely different type of audience. It is a fast-paced, no-nonsense crowd with a very short attention span. People are hungry for information, greedy for instant results, and vocal about their expectations. Speakers, therefore, need new tools and techniques to satisfy these demanding circumstances. This book is for speakers addressing a twenty-first-century audience.

This book has another important purpose. In today's fast-paced world, most of us don't have time to read voluminous books filled with elaborate discussions, so you want to get the best value for the time you spend reading. You are the kind of reader we had in mind. This is an inclusive guide that is easy and fast to read. It consists of 20 chapters, each loaded with practical easy-to-follow tips. There is no continuity between the chapters. You may wish to read these "independent" essays in sequence or selectively choose those that strike your greatest interest.

We ourselves have successfully used the techniques presented herein. We have also taught them to several of our clients who have obtained the results they wanted with their audiences. We hope you will benefit from our experience as well. Please feel free to write or email us with your thoughts, ideas, and feedback. We would like to hear from you!

PSK
SMM

140 S. Dearborn Street, Suite 411
Chicago, Illinois 60603
mail@kodukula.com
www.kodukula.com

1. TOP 10 TIPS

1. **Make it about them, not about you.** This is the Number 1 secret of outstanding speakers and trainers. Your presentation should focus on your audience rather than on you. It should address *their* needs and challenges. From the moment you walk into the presentation room until the moment you say good-bye, the focus of your presentation should be on them. Let's face it: In most cases, your audience members haven't even heard your name before they showed up in the room—unless you are a celebrity speaker. They are there because of their own needs. It's your job to find out what those needs are and provide help.

   For starters, here is a tip: Increase your UIQ. UIQ (you–I coefficient) is the ratio of how many times the pronouns *you* and *I* are used in a presentation. If yours is more than 30 (30 *you*s to one *I*), welcome to the Speakers' MENSA Club! (Don't start writing checks for membership; the club is only imaginary.)

Larry King of CNN, known as King of Talk, recently commented on his show: "It isn't about me; it's about them." Whether you are talking on TV or speaking in public, the principle is the same. It will make you a winner every time—time after time in the future!

2.   **Fire 'em up with five I's.** Imagine a pyramid with five steps representing these five I's in the ascending order: information, involvement, ideas, insight, and inspiration. Mediocre speakers remain stuck toward the bottom I's of the hierarchy, whereas the best-in-class take their audience to the top every time. Excelling in one area is not good enough. You must

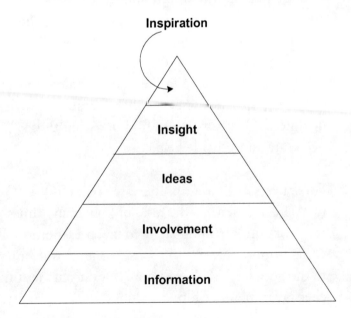

be a decathlon champion and stretch to work your way to the top. As a speaker, you must provide valuable information; as a facilitator, involve them; as a practitioner of your craft, you must give them great practical ideas; as a philosopher, you must share your insights; and as a leader, you must inspire them to reach new heights. All this will ultimately help you reach new heights in your own career.

3. **Create value.** You have been asked to speak for a reason. *You* are the expert, the top performer, the leader. Most people in the audience want "take aways" from your talk. What advice can you give them? What practical tools can you impart? Offer explicit solutions to their problems as opposed to vague textbook explanations. Give them tangible ideas and tips they can start using immediately with little or no tweaking required.

4. **Connect with your audience.** Choreographing your movement and emotion with your message is vital to connecting with your audience. This means you must deliver your message with body, mind, and heart; a talent Nick Morgan, Harvard Management Communications Letter Editor, calls "kinesthetic" speaking. While mediocre presenters are good at connecting intellectually and physically, it takes a maestro to make an emotional connection.

Connectivity establishes trust and helps build a stronger bond with your listeners. Make this special connection and they will believe your words and easily forgive your *faux pas*.

5. **Build bold "bookends."** Bookends are the opening and closing of your presentations. The opening sets the tone for what's to come and the closing tells your listeners where to go and what to do next. Make them **bold**—not boring. Begin with a bang to seize listener interest. Use a motivational story, a powerful anecdote, a humorous tale, congratulatory comments, or an intriguing statement. Give your audience a flavor for your style, a sense of what they may expect later, and make them feel comfortable.

   When closing, on the other hand, do more than just highlight key points: Return to your opening and tie all of your ideas together. End the talk on a high note. Customer service research shows that the closing experience for the customer is most memorable. At the end, seize the opportunity to make a long-lasting positive impact on your audience. Do you close with a simple "Thank you"? *Bo-ring!* Make it **bold!**

6. **Perform with pizzazz.** In today's world of *Oprah*, most of us want to be "edutained" and "infotained." Especially with an increasing presence

of the MTV generation in the workforce, your speaking techniques need to grab and sustain your audience's attention. Television has changed the rules. The audience needs some sort of "pizzazz" every seven minutes. Entertainment may not be your cup of tea, but your audience expects an Oscar-worthy presentation.

Speakers with pizzazz are *savoir-faire* storytellers. They tell succinct, dramatic stories with vivid images and choreographed animation. The larger the audience, the more animated you must be. Images and animation not only create interest and hold attention, but they also improve understanding and provide inspiration. Professor Cynthia Emrich of Purdue University, who has studied the speaking styles of U.S. presidents, recommends the use of image-based words—such as *hand, grow,* and *path*—versus abstract, concept-based words—such as *help, produce,* and *alternative.* Punctuate your presentation with potent punch lines and sound bytes. Always pause after making a powerful point. Use smooth transitions, much like a television news anchor does, as you move from one topic to the next. Animation is key to your performance.

7. **Energize the environment.** Like a rock star in a concert stadium, you need to keep your audience

energized constantly. This is much easier for short motivational talks and other presentations than it is for a three-day training program. The key is to be energetic and enthusiastic yourself. Establish the pace and energy level from the moment you greet your audience at the door or on the platform. Speak loudly and relatively fast—but vary the pace; even Mick Jagger sings ballads in between the rock-and-roll numbers.

Maintain the energy level by creating multisensory stimulations using audio, visual, and kinesthetic means. Be positive. Avoid negativity. Show your passion. Tell motivational stories. Use humor. Do magic. Play music. Show videos. Sing. Dance. "Wait," you say, "that's showbiz." That's right! We're talking about edutainment.

8. **Customize content.** Wouldn't you love to wear and look terrific in a custom-tailored suit as opposed to off-the-shelf garb—especially if the price is right? The key to customizing your presentation is speaking the same language as your listeners and addressing their needs. Based on prior experience and advance research, you probably know the *lingua franca* of the collective audience. But how about knowing and *using* the audience's specific dialects? Spend time with them, ask the right

questions before you start the presentation, and
continue to ask them throughout the speech,
especially if it is a long one. Egocentric speakers
with low UIQs (see Tip No. 1 in this chapter)
spend much of their time talking about themselves,
while star performers spend more time actively
learning about the audience's needs, experiences,
and expectations. Advance homework is necessary
here, otherwise you will need to get to your venue
early so you can spend time with your audience
practicing your JIT (just-in-time) learning skills.

9.   **Master the material.** This may be a no-brainer, but
it is of paramount importance. You will gain
enormous credibility if you demonstrate your
thorough knowledge of and vast experience in the
topic while making it easy to understand for your
audience. You will gain even more points by sharing
interesting insights based on your knowledge from
general business/management areas, arts, science,
history, philosophy, pop culture, etc. Quote
business gurus, thinkers, and philosophers the
audience knows and respects, and use examples
from current books, magazines, and trade journals.

10. **Be yourself.** Richard Haas, who wrote many
speeches for President George Bush, the senior,
learned early on that oratory was as welcomed by

his boss as a second helping of broccoli. Align your presentation style with your personality. Never try to be someone you are not. In doing so, you are cheating yourself and risking a loss of integrity. Without integrity, you will be like a skyscraper in the Windy City with no foundation! Don't copy someone else's style. Let your own personality come through. Most important, no matter what you do to dazzle your audience, be genuine! And be yourself!

2. DO YOU KNOW YOUR CUSTOMERS?

1. **Know thy customer.** This is a well-known truism, yet few businesspeople *really* know their customers. Your customers for a given assignment primarily consist of the audience attending your presentation, your host, your primary customer contact, and the sponsoring organization. Remember Tip No. 1 from Chapter 1? *Make it about them, not about you.* It is imperative that you know who your customers are in the first place. Make sure you use the exact name of the team, group, association, organization, etc., that is sponsoring your presentation.

2. **Know more than the name.** Do homework on your customer or the sponsoring organization and get to know about their business, services, products, owners, executives, company history, corporate mission, organizational structure, major initiatives currently underway (for example, mergers/ acquisitions), and so on. Familiarize yourself with your customer's culture. This may involve a little bit

of your time, but it is important. Start with the organization's website. Ask your host, customer contact, and representative audience members numerous questions. Talk to your customer's customers. Research the organization and their industry with help from books, business journals, trade magazines, etc. The more you know about the organization, the more credibility you will establish with your customers, and ultimately the more effective you will be in serving their needs.

3.   **Know your audience.** Get to know the names of as many individuals in your audience as possible before you start your presentation. If possible, get a list of participants and their job titles in advance, or make every attempt to get to know them as you "meet and greet" before the presentation. Find out:

- how exactly each individual's name is pronounced

- what their jobs are

- the level of their work experience

- their educational background

- the gender and ethnic make-up of the group

- how long they have been with the organization

- whether they know each other

- whether they are meeting each other for the first time

- their current challenges

- what advance information they received about your presentation

- what results they expect from your presentation

- whether there are other programs preceding and succeeding yours, and if yes, what they are

- the level of audience knowledge and skill in the subject you will be discussing

- whether they are coming to see you on their day off (e.g. Saturday)

- whether participation in your presentation is mandatory or voluntary

- whether they paid to hear you speak

- whether they heard you speak before

4.   **Turn knowledge into action.** Weave skillfully the knowledge you gained about your customers into the content and message of your presentation. Here are some tips that will help you:

- Mention the name of the customer organization frequently.

- Quote statements from their corporate executives and state their names.

- Congratulate the group on any successes they may have recently enjoyed.

- Refer to history, trends, challenges, successes, etc., of their industry as a whole.

- Use individual participants' names frequently. For example, when presenting a case study, instead of using fictitious names, use the names of individuals in the audience whenever appropriate. Be sure not to offend anyone. To initiate a discussion on a particular issue or challenge, you may start by saying *"Let's say our friend Peter here is faced with…"* and make the discussion personal.

- Offer solutions to problems of specific individuals in the audience and mention their names when appropriate.

- Thank the host, your customer contact, and the audience either in your opening or in your closing remarks.

- Make sure you have met not only the formal objectives of your program but also the expectations of your audience.

"Spoon feeding, in the long run, teaches us nothing but the shape of the spoon."

—*E. M. Forster*

3. BOLD BEGINNINGS

1. **Begin with a bang.** The audience will make decisions about you, your topic, and their level of commitment to your presentation in less than two minutes. Your opening will set the tone and pace of your talk, and it will give the audience a hint of what is to come. It is a snapshot of your style and personality. **Make it bold.**

2. **Start with a high energy level.** Start on a high note with positive energy. Show your passion and enthusiasm for your subject and your job. No one enjoys presenters or trainers who act like they don't particularly like what they are doing. This is especially disheartening to audiences that are "made" to sit through your presentation or training.

3. **Make a great first impression.** Dress appropriately. Make sure your hair is out of your face and wear only a minimal amount of jewelry. Walk confidently to the podium or to the front of the

venue, plant your feet, take a deep breath, and make eye contact with your audience before you begin to speak. Start with a smile. Avoid being busy with last-minute details right before your presentation. Appear calm, organized, and excited to be there.

4.   **Set norms early.** Within the first four minutes of your presentation, you will create audience expectations. If you want audience involvement, laughter, etc., give them a taste in your opening comments. Many a speaker is challenged when, after talking for 45 minutes straight, the audience won't interact or participate in an activity. Why? The norm has been clearly set: I, the speaker, talk; you, the audience, listen.

5.   **State key objectives.** In a keynote address, you will typically make from one to three points, which you should mention near the beginning of your talk. In a training session, state the formal objectives of the program, and be sure to ask the participants what their expectations are.

6.   **Start on time.** Punctuality speaks for itself. It shows you are disciplined and organized. Unless there is a compelling reason, never start late. If you were to start late, announce it early on so your audience

knows. Nobody likes to sit in an airport without knowing when they will be boarded to take off.

7.   **Add value from the start.** You can win your audience from the start, when you add value from the start. You may do this by presenting an important statistic that matters to them, providing a solution to one of their known problems, conducting a quick learning activity, etc.

8.   **Do not break off your opening.** Do not stop in the middle of your opening to address other distracting business such as seating of late arrivers. Interruptions rob you of your momentum, energy, and excitement. Finish your opening and then address any other needs.

9.   **Use icebreakers.** Create a situation in which your audience can meet other participants in an interesting way, perhaps using a game or a riddle. Get them up moving around and talking to each other. This also creates energy within the group.

10.   **Limit your opening to four minutes**. Unseasoned presenters often make their openings too long. This most likely will lead to a loss of audience interest. Also, long openings shorten the precious time you could use for the topic at hand.

11. **Examples.** Here are some common examples for openings:

- A story related to yourself, somebody you know, an anonymous person, a business, or a universal event like the Olympics.

- A joke.

- An interesting question.

- A startling visual or a statistic.

- A relevant metaphor or analogy.

- Drama: A robbery during a security class or a skit showing serious (or funny) workplace frustrations for a stress-management class.

- "Reverse modeling," showing the *wrong way* to do something. (This usually makes the audience laugh, and you can get interaction by asking them what was wrong with the picture.)

12. **Make it bold, not boring.** Do not start your presentation with "Thank you for…." Other boring beginnings include the weather, the venue, and your lost baggage at the airport.

4. WHAT ADULTS WANT

1.   **Understand needs.** Adults are motivated to learn primarily based on their needs. If they have a problem to solve in their personal or professional lives, they are even more interested. Unless you are hired to simply entertain your audience (perhaps as a comedian), or you are a celebrity speaker (in which case your audience members are most interested in telling everybody they know "I saw so-and-so"), you *must* understand what they need. Therefore, find out in advance what their needs are and focus on ways to satisfy them.

2.   **Investigate needs.** Before discovering their needs, first know who your audience members are. (See Chapter 2.) Spend time talking to your host, sponsor, customer contact, a few representatives from your audience, or even your customer's customers far in advance of your presentation. Find out what their current needs, challenges, and

priorities are and what they expect to gain from your presentation or training.

3. **Start early.** Understanding the audience's needs is a continuous process that should start on the day you have accepted the assignment. There may never be an end to this process as long as you want to work with this customer. Make every attempt to know your audience's needs immediately prior to, during, and even *after* your presentation.

4. **Focus on the present.** Children usually learn for the future, but adults want information they can use *now*. Therefore, focus on the solutions to their present challenges.

5. **Less theory and more "real" world!** Although many adults are interested in basic theory, the most important reason they come to hear you is to discuss and find solutions to their day-to-day problems at work or in their personal lives. Avoid elaborate theoretical discourses.

6. **Engage in various "modalities."** Adults learn through several media, including visual, audio, and tactile modes. They get bored easily with the use of just one medium. Knowingly or unknowingly, most adults have either one or two primary modalities. In

order to cater to every adult in your audience, it is vital that you vary your means of communication using several different media (Chapters 7 and 11) and learning techniques (Chapter 6).

7. **Use a variety of learning techniques.** Historically, lecture or narration may have been the most common form of speech or training, but today's audiences demand far more. They want to do more than just listen. Participation and interaction is vital to today's adult audience. There are many simple techniques that make adult learning extremely effective:

- Use the "Socratic" method by asking questions, and build your presentation on the answers. Occasionally pose rhetorical questions to stimulate thinking.

- Make your audience curious by using "hooks."

- Spice up your presentation with humor (Chapter 10), stories, statistics, studies, etc. (Chapter 7).

- Employ hands-on exercises (Chapter 9), including case studies, brainstorming sessions, role-playing exercises, games, etc.

- Don't always just impart knowledge. Let your "students" learn through "self-discovery," an effective learning method for some adults.

Irrespective of the techniques you use, don't forget to connect the activities involved with the learning objectives.

8. **Make everybody a teacher.** Your audience can learn not only from you but also from their peers. Create opportunities for group interactions where everybody can become a teacher.

9. **Show expertise.** Adults prefer to learn from experts. It is vital to your success that you become an expert in your subject matter. Furthermore, you can shine by gaining and sharing knowledge from other areas as well. Don't take your credibility with the audience for granted just because your résumé is as long as a Stephen King novel. It will evaporate quickly if you don't demonstrate your qualifications in your presentation. Take every opportunity to flaunt your expertise during the whole encounter.

10. **Pour passion.** Adults are inspired by passionate people. Show your sincere passion for the subject you are talking about, as well as for helping people in the audience to do better in their lives. Your

passion expresses itself when you love what you do and do what you love.

11. **Minimize lecturing.** In training sessions, do not "lecture" for more than 10 minutes at a time. Intersperse the lecture with different activities and exercises.

12. **Provide plenty of breaks.** Adult brains need breaks from learning every 60 to 90 minutes or so. In long training sessions, give frequent breaks and use "energizers" to keep the attention sharp.

13. **Show empathy.** Most adults are thrilled when they can take away from your presentation something tangible that will help them make their personal or professional lives better. On the other hand, they will be upset if you act as if they are broken, and you "the almighty" have come to save them from their misery. Therefore, it is vital that you empathize with them, show them you have "been there and done that," and then offer solutions. This will help you make an emotional connection and establish "likeability" with your audience, which according to Bert Decker, a well-known communications expert, is key to the success of a speaker.

14.   **Don't be condescending.** Adults relate their
      learning to their previous experience and often
      define themselves by what they know. Never put
      down their previous experience or an older
      technology or practice they have been used to. It
      will be discouraging or insulting to the adult
      learner. Some adults may have difficulty
      "unlearning" or may resist change. This type of
      behavior may seem negative, but is often just a sign
      of a lack of confidence. You need to provide
      encouragement.

15.   **Avoid a "parental" tone.** Always treat your
      audience members as adults and with dignity and
      respect.

16.   **Keep time commitments.** Adults are irritated when
      time commitments are not kept. Always start on
      time and finish on or before schedule. Never go
      beyond your designated finish time. If you require
      extra time, show a valid reason for extending your
      presentation, and always get permission in advance
      from your audience.

17.   **Plan time for Q & A.** Always save time for
      questions and answers (Q & A) at the very end of
      your presentation. It is more important that you
      address at least a majority of, if not all, audience

questions than it is to finish your planned agenda. If you are rushed for time, cut short on the content, but do not compromise on Q & A!

18. **Be flexible.** Adult learners enjoy self-direction and flexibility, and do not want to be controlled. Don't try to force an agenda on them simply because you have planned it. Don't repeatedly make them wait for answers to their questions simply because it doesn't fit your schedule. Answer their questions promptly. Give them choices. Be flexible.

19. **Do not read from notes.** Need we say more?

"Don't just learn the tricks of the trade. Learn the trade."

—*James Bennis*

5. LET'S GET PHYSICAL!

1. **Choreograph movement with message.** The choreography of your body movement with your message will help you make an emotional connection with your audience, which is a key ingredient of your success. What you do with your physical image—eyes, voice, posture, hand gestures, and body movement—can inject passion, energy, and dynamism into your presentation and transcend it to a higher level. This can be a make-or-break factor for your success as a speaker.

2. **Start with your image.** In today's world, where the image of the rumple-clothed, absent-minded professor is nearly gone, the audience expects you to look "professional." While "image" is primarily a personal matter, here are some basic tips:

    *   Dress appropriately for the occasion. Ask your host or customer contact in advance what they expect you to wear. Usually it is best to dress at

the level of the audience or one notch above that. Wear clean, pressed clothes. (Always dress "business casual" when flying, so even if your luggage is lost, you have decent clothes for your presentation.)

- Wear solid colors. Avoid large stripes or anything the audience might find distracting.

- Let the audience see your eyes. Avoid dark glasses, and if you must wear eyeglasses, use glare-proof lenses whenever possible.

- Keep your fingernails trimmed and clean. No chipped nail polish.

- Wear accessories conservatively. Shy away from bold jewelry.

- Check your teeth and breath if you are speaking after lunch. Use mints frequently.

- Keep your shoes neat and clean.

3. **Make eye contact.** Use eye contact to engage your audience. Look into the eyes of individuals and speak as if you were talking directly to them one-on-one. Hold each gaze for two to four seconds.

A good time to break eye contact is at the end of a sentence. Avoid "cocktail party" eyes—those that look all around the audience but not in their eyes.

4. **Uncover your "blind spot."** Every speaker or trainer has a spot (maybe more than one) in the audience they neglect. Some look over the front row, some ignore people in the back, some disregard the back corners. Make sure you cover the entire audience. You may divide the audience into sections in an imaginary grid and go from one section to another to cover the entire group.

5. **Use the power of your voice.** Some of the best-known speakers (e.g., Dr. Martin Luther King, Jr., President John F. Kennedy) turned their moving messages into motivational mantras with the power of their voice. By varying voice inflections and cadence, you can turn ordinary words into compelling mental images that can create interest and maintain attention and excitement within your audience. Here are some tips on how you can accomplish this:

- Speak clearly. Don't mumble.

- Avoid using a monotone voice. To practice variety in tone and inflection, read a passage much like the storytelling lady at the local library would.

- Lower the tone of your voice. It projects credibility.

- Vary your vocal intensity, as well as the rhythm and rate of your speech.

- When telling a story, start slowly and build speed.

- Slow down to emphasize a point.

- Pause (3 to 4 seconds) after an interesting insight or a powerful message.

- Avoid "you knows" and "ahs."

- Do not chew gum while speaking.

- Do not drink carbonated beverages before or during presentations.

6. **Stand up straight.** You have heard this from your mother ever since you were little. Practice the "walk away from the wall" technique: Stand against the wall with your feet and shoulders touching the wall

and walk away from it. Do not slouch. Avoid leaning on one leg and throwing your hip out, or leaning on the lectern or the equipment. Keep your elbows away from your waist and open up.

7. **Do not hide.** Do not allow barriers, such as lecterns, projection equipment, tables, etc., to come between you and your audience. Move away from the lectern unless you are giving a "formal" speech. If you need a microphone, make sure you have a lavaliere type that gives you the freedom to move around. (More on microphones in Chapter 12.)

8. **Do not hide your hands.** Avoid putting your hands in your pockets, behind you, or in front of you in a "fig leaf" position. Use your hands constantly for emphasis. Extend them forward or sideways for open gestures. Empty your pockets before you start speaking in order to avoid playing with your pocket change or keys. Do not hold pens, papers, or pointers for longer than necessary. These can create distractions and reveal any signs of your anxiety.

9. **Make bigger gestures with bigger audiences.** Amplify your gestures as the size of the audience increases.

10. **Avoid repetitive or distracting gestures.** An example of a repetitive gesture is pushing up

eyeglasses. Annoying gestures include playing with your hair or jewelry or clicking a pen.

11. **Face the audience.** Avoid showing your back to the audience, especially while you are speaking. Even when using visual aids, do not turn your back to the audience; a common mistake made by even the most experienced speakers. Maintain eye contact with the participants. Don't talk to the screen or read from it. Know your visuals (for example, slides) well enough so you won't need to read from them. For highlighting points on the screen using a pointer, stand at an angle or turn your upper body at an angle. (See Chapters 11, 12, and 13 on audio-visual matters.)

12. **Do not become a "statue."** Avoid standing in one position for extended periods unless you are talking from behind a lectern for a "formal" speech. Move freely and slowly about the space in front of the audience or on the platform if there is one. When moving to the left of your audience, stop and turn slightly diagonally to the right and vice versa. After a powerful point, an insightful idea, or a spicy sound byte, stand straight for three to four seconds with what is called the "power pause."

13. **Do not pace.** Continuous pacing irritates the audience. You may move from place to place slowly,

but plant yourself first before moving again. Also, avoid "rocking" back and forth on your toes and heels. This is another distraction to the audience.

14. **Practice and progress.** Rehearse your speech using a video camera. Play it back and improve your performance by self-critique and self-correction. Furthermore, practice in front of a mentor or a colleague and receive objective feedback. All this may be painful, but the results will be worth it. If the three laws of real estate are location, location, and location, the three laws of presentations are preparation, preparation, and preparation.

"Tell me, I'll forget.
Show me, I'll remember.
Involve me, I'll understand."

—*Confucius*

6. ENHANCING RETENTION

1. **Repeat, repeat, repeat.** Research shows that 50 percent of what we learn in a seminar is forgotten in two days and 95 percent is forgotten after a week. Enhancing retention should be a key objective of every presentation or training program. Repetition is the easiest path to retention. Find ways to repeat key points as often as possible. In a long training session, conduct multiple reviews. Typically adults need 5 to 7 repetitions to ensure awareness, let alone long-term retention.

2. **Repeat.**

3. **Use all three modalities.** Visual: Show it. Audio: Say it or describe in detail. Tactile: Do it and let them do it. Use different types of exercises to help your audience learn and practice the new skill or knowledge.

4.   **Create a common theme.** Weave a common thread throughout your presentation and keep tying different concepts together.

5.   **Encourage writing.** Encourage people to take notes. When making key points, you may preface by saying: *"You may want to write this down."* Note-taking helps with retention, even if you never refer to the notes.

6.   **Promote goal setting.** Have the participants set goals at the end of your presentation. This helps them focus on the real needs and follow through. Get them to commit to building one or two new habits.

7.   **Extract information.** Instead of giving the information yourself, ask questions as much as you can to extract information. Guide and prompt before telling.

8.   **Involve audience.** The more they participate, the more they retain. (See Chapter 8, "Energizing Your Audience.")

9.   **Use acronyms and sound bytes.** These are easy to remember. The catchier they are, the longer the audience's retention is. Who can forget: Franklin D. Roosevelt's Depression-era message, "The only

thing we have to fear is fear itself"? John F. Kennedy's inaugural appeal, "Ask not what your country can do for you…"? Lyndon B. Johnson's catchphrase, "Great Society"?

10. **Use visual aids often.** Take advantage of a variety of aids. Don't just stick with one. In addition to slides and flip charts, use appropriate props.

11. **Build exercises around key points.** Create opportunities to apply key lessons learned through a variety of exercises.

12. **Spice up your presentation.** Add metaphors, analogies, statistics, powerful stories, jokes, etc., for making your presentation more colorful and interesting. This ultimately helps with retention.

13. **Use game show formats for reviews.** Conduct reviews using famous TV game show formats such as *Who Wants to Be a Millionaire* and *Jeopardy!* This will add entertainment and a sense of fun to your program.

14. **Make it fun.** Create a fun atmosphere where learning is enhanced.

15. **See Chapter 4, "What Adults Want."**

"If a man empties his purse into his head, no one can take it from him."

—*Ben Franklin*

7. "IT'S THE EDUTAINMENT, STUPID!"

1. **Engage in edutainment.** In today's MTV world, the attention span of children as well as of adults is going south like the stock market in 2000. So how do you keep your audience interested, attentive, and focused on your message? The answer lies in *education through entertainment.* We are not talking about performing in a Spielberg movie, so don't lose your hope of speaking in front of an audience.

2. **Loosen up!** For starters, forget hiding behind the lectern (or some such cover) with your hands in your pocket, cocktail-eyes rolling all over the audience, and words rolling out in a monotone voice. Welcome to the *Oprah* world: Get in front of the audience, directly in their face! (See Chapter 5 on eye contact, voice, body movement, and image.)

3. **Cultivate charisma.** Who said Presidents Jack Kennedy and Bill Clinton were the *only* owners of charisma? Just ask Dr. Tony Alessandra, the author

of *Charisma*, a 1997 book published by McGraw-Hill. Contrary to the popular belief that it is inborn, charisma can be learned. You don't think you have it? Go get it! Stand straight. Smile. Laugh. Show confidence. Exude enthusiasm. Think positive. Be interested in others. Listen more…. That's just for starters!

4.   **Spice it up every seven minutes.** Spice up your presentation with interesting stories, studies, statistics, humor, quotes, analogies, metaphors, etc., at least every seven minutes. This will not only make your presentation more interesting, but it will also help the audience understand the content better and retain it longer.

5.   **Sprinkle in sound bytes.** Before you start rolling your eyes, think about what people *really* remember at the end of the day. You remember, of course, "Where's the beef?" as asked by 1986 presidential candidate Walter Mondale. "Read my lips, no new taxes!" promised another presidential candidate, George H. W. Bush. "Greed is good," confessed Gordon Gecko of *Wall Street.* The civil-rights leader Dr. Martin Luther King, Jr., inspired a whole generation with "I have a dream." (Okay, maybe King belongs to a different league than the rest.)

Prepare in advance and use catchphrases and sound bytes to add pizzazz to your presentation.

6. **Become a savvy storyteller.** Great communicators are great storytellers. First, find relevant stories. They are ubiquitous. You just have to be alert. Collect as many stories as you can, both business and family related. Practice presenting them. Make them interesting. Make them powerful. Show passion. Inject animation. Use drama. Create suspense. Patricia Fripp, a well-known speech coach, recommends what she calls the "I've got a secret to tell you" approach to storytelling.

7. **Think and link.** Every day we come across many stories, jokes, statistics, and studies, but most of us do not remember them. It is good practice to collect, catalogue, and store these anecdotes for future use. When it is time to prepare for a new speech or a training session, you will already have a wealth of information. Now it is time to think and link the stories you have to the message you want to deliver.

8. **Keep them concise.** Limit each story or joke to two minutes, otherwise people will lose interest. Remember their attention span! Don't test their patience. Furthermore, limit yourself to one story, one joke, or one study at a time in order to make a

point. Do not bury your main point in a myriad of stories. Use the P.E.P. formula. *P:* Point; *E:* Example; *P:* Point repeated. Make your point, give an example, and then repeat the point. Then move on.

9.   **Be authentic.** Check your facts and figures. One humorist once said that 68 percent of all statistics are incorrect! Provide references for your stories, studies, and statistics (title, author's name, publication year, etc.). Never present somebody else's quote, story, or work as your own. Don't say it happened to you if it didn't. Even a single mistake in this area will make one wonder about the authenticity of your entire message. Playing with credibility is like playing with fire. It may destroy your career.

10. **Avoid autobiography.** Few speakers engage in autobiographical presentations where they spend excessive time talking about themselves. This is okay if you are Nelson Mandela and people are interested in hearing about you. From the rest of us, however, the audience wants to learn about topics other than ourselves.

11. **Make it relevant.** It is vital that you make your stories and jokes relevant to the point you are trying

to make. Otherwise the audience will feel that you are not giving them value, but are wasting their time. If the relevance is not too obvious, you may say: *"The reason I tell this story is ...,"* and make your point. Try to use information that directly relates to your audience's industry and business. If you have a mixed audience, vary the types of examples.

12. **Use variety.** You may organize your speech, and especially your training session, as a series of acts in a play. Make each act different and unique by creating diverse "sets," bringing in various "characters," using assorted themes, and adding multiple colors. Interaction. Exercises. Stories. Sound bytes. Jokes. Laughter. Song. Dance. Magic. And more!

"To know and not to do is not to know."

—*Leo Buscaglia*

8. ENERGIZING YOUR AUDIENCE

1. **Fire up.** John Wesley, preacher and founder of
    Methodism, was asked how he was able to attract
    huge crowds to his sermons. His answer: "I just set
    myself on fire, and people come from miles to
    watch me burn." Think about how you can set
    yourself on fire—metaphorically speaking, of
    course.

2. **Radiate enthusiasm.** Here is a simple rule to create
    enthusiasm in your audience: Be enthusiastic
    yourself. From the minute you walk into the
    presentation venue until you say goodbye, never let
    your enthusiasm down. "Being enthusiastic isn't
    merely talking energetically and gesturing wildly
    about your passion," says Dr. Tony Alessandra,
    bestselling author of *Charisma*. "Your enthusiasm
    can be revealed by the earnestness and persistence
    with which you seek to get others involved. It can
    be shown by your strength of commitment, your
    refusal to become discouraged, that spark in your

eye, that warm smile, and the unmistakable genuineness that emanates from you as you explain, again and again, your mission."

3. **Begin with a bang.** As discussed in Chapter 3, start on a high note. Tell a powerful inspirational story. Have a highly interactive, game-oriented, competitive icebreaker. Play fast, upbeat music. Get everybody to laugh very loud!

4. **Enhance audience participation.** Do everything possible to get audience members to interact with you as well as with each other as a whole group or in subgroups. You may use icebreakers, games, team-based assignments, role-playing exercises, and various other activities.

5. **Set the norms early on.** If you want audience participation, you must create the opportunity for it within the first few minutes of your presentation. You may do this by asking questions. Announce up front that you will ask numerous questions and tell them it's all right if they don't know the answers or give incorrect responses.

6. **Ask questions frequently.** Examples of generic questions include: *"Does this make sense?" "How does it make sense?" "What's your experience in this area?"*

"What problems have you faced doing this?" "Can you give me a real-world example on this?" "Any questions on what we have covered so far?" When asking these types of questions, it is preferable not to call upon specific individuals. Leave the discussion open to the entire group. If you make it a practice to call upon anyone at anytime, be sure to tell everyone up front that this is a possibility. One way to call directly upon a person is to call her name first, and then ask the question, so she will be better prepared to listen.

7. **Ask stimulating questions.** Pose questions that make people think. Don't ask tough questions all the time. A good rule to follow is that at least 90 percent of the questions should be answerable. Give credit for partial answers. If they don't get it right the first time, guide them toward the right answer, perhaps by asking more questions.

8. **Create a multisensory experience.** Play upbeat music and/or show music video clips before starting the presentation and during the breaks.

9. **Use energizers.** Intersperse your presentation with games and other stimulating exercises. Create opportunities where participants can use both their right and left brains. Make sure that they have

enough time to complete the exercises. Also, don't let them sit idly for too long.

10.   **Reward results.** According to Michael LeBoeuf, author and management consultant, the greatest management principle in the world is: "You get what you reward." Therefore, reward desired results. The reward may simply be acknowledging a job well done or it can be something more tangible.

11.   **Affirm your audience.** Don't be the type of speaker who makes the audience feel "broken" and as if they need to be fixed. They are where they are, and you will help them move to the next level.

12.   **Don't talk slowly.** An average person speaks at a rate of 125 to 150 words per minute. To keep the energy level high, you may need to speak at a higher speed. However, it is not a good idea to speak fast all the time, so vary your speed. Make sure you avoid talking too slowly.

9. EXERCISE EXCELLENCE

1. **Pack your program with exercises.** This is most applicable to training. Use a variety of exercises, such as small-group discussions, case studies, brainstorming, games, role-playing exercises, and mini-projects. Exercises help break the long lectures into smaller doses, and, more important, they facilitate better understanding and longer retention of knowledge. Furthermore, they help your trainees start developing new skills. Below are tips applicable to most exercises:

    *   Pack more exercises in the afternoon particularly between 1:30 and 3:30.

    *   Build exercises directly related to the learning objectives.

    *   State clearly up front the objectives and/or the expected outcomes of the exercise.

- Briefly go over any reading materials provided.

- Write any rules (as in games) clearly on a flip chart and post them.

- Set time limits.

- Provide just enough time to complete the exercise. Do not give excess time.

- Make the exercise challenging.

- At least two times during the exercise, preferably toward the latter part, let the participants know how much time they have left for completion.

- Check with the trainees early on during the exercise to make sure they understand the objectives and are on the right track.

- Make sure every team finishes the exercise. They will be disappointed and frustrated if they don't. You may have to guide the slow teams toward the finish line.

- Always have a debriefing session on the exercise.

- Set a time limit for debriefing as well.

- Give a chance for all groups to share their results.

10. HUMOROUS ENCOUNTERS

1. **Don't tell jokes if it's not your cup of tea.** First, don't feel like you *have* to tell jokes. Many people feel like they must start a presentation with a joke. No rules call for it. There are plenty of outstanding speakers who do not tell jokes. Conversely, there are excellent joke tellers who are mediocre speakers. Your joke-telling skill is not a measure of your speaking or training ability. If you are not comfortable telling jokes, simply don't!

2. **Add humor.** Humor is different from telling jokes. For humor, you may prepare in advance, but it works best when it is spontaneous. A good rule for humor is: If it is funny when you *read* it, you can most likely recite it and present it humorously. Self-deprecating humor works well for most people. Just be sure to establish credibility first. Asked how he became a war hero, President John F. Kennedy responded, "It was involuntary. They sank my boat."

3. **Do not use politically incorrect humor.** Making fun of a specific gender, group, nationality, or

religion is not a good idea in our age of political correctness. Here is a simple rule to decide whether you want to use a joke or a story: If you have any doubts about it, don't use it.

4.   **Avoid "put down" humor.** "Put down" humor toward the audience is not received well. It may work well with a heckler, as long as it is light.

5.   **Test your jokes first.** Try your jokes on friends or colleagues first in an informal environment to see if they are acceptable and funny. This also gives you practice and ideas for improvement.

6.   **Make jokes short.** The shorter the better. Follow a two-minute rule. Listeners lose interest as the joke gets longer. Also, the longer the joke, the funnier it is expected to be, and so your audience's patience should be rewarded.

7.   **Repeat the point after using humor.** Information immediately *after* humor is not easily retained by the audience and should be repeated.

8.   **Continuously update your jokes.** Audiences don't appreciate jokes they already have heard. Too many old jokes indicate that you are not current and not keeping abreast. If you were to tell an old joke, make sure it has new significance. You may tell such a joke by prefacing: *"This may be a joke you have heard, but it has a new meaning...."*

11. MEDIA MATTERS

1. **Use the right media for the right occasion.**
    Investigate in advance the size and the makeup of
    your audience, the layout of the presentation room,
    and the presentation media available to you. Then
    evaluate and decide on what audio/visual (AV)
    means would work best. Standard nonelectronic
    media include flip charts and white boards, while
    electronic media include overhead projection
    (OHP), LCD (liquid crystal display) projection for
    slides, and TV for motion picture. (OHP slides are
    often referred to as transparencies.)

    White boards and flip charts are commonly found
    in training rooms and are effective for small groups
    of less than 30 people. OHP and video are
    universally available, are most commonly used, and
    work well for both small and large groups. LCD
    projection is catching on slowly, as laptops loaded
    with Microsoft's PowerPoint® (software for creating
    slides) are becoming ubiquitous. Use of DVD for
    motion pictures will probably become common

within the next decade as it becomes easier to burn your own DVDs. LCD slides and DVDs are relatively more sophisticated and highly recommended for any size audience.

2.	**Avoid overhead projectors.** They are low-tech, unsophisticated, and cumbersome. Use them only if necessary. Their advantages, however, include portability, ease of operation, universal availability, and low cost. If LCD projection is unavailable, OHP may be your only choice. Even with LCD availability, you may consider OHP for drawing pictures for large audiences where flip charts would be too small and PowerPoint® is not conducive to free hand drawing. Plus, *always* have an OHP as a back-up to the LCD.

3.	**Make media hassle-free.** The evening of September 22, 1993, as he started to address a joint session of the Congress of the United States with millions of Americans watching on television, President Bill Clinton noticed that the text in the TelePrompTer was the wrong speech. For seven minutes—seven long minutes—the president improvised most brilliantly until his aides finally got the right speech in the machine and then transitioned seamlessly. Whereas only a maestro like Clinton can make such a mishap totally inconspicuous, the whole experience can be nerve-wracking for most of us amateurs. The answer to making presentation media work smoothly for you is advance preparation. If time permits, check the equipment and try it the day or night before the presentation. Otherwise, get to the venue far in advance the day of your talk. Hassling with the equipment as the audience is coming into the room is not good practice. You want to use that precious time for "meeting and greeting." Here are a few tips for preparing in advance with the AV equipment:

- Test the equipment to ensure operability.

- Know how to operate the equipment yourself. Familiarize yourself with equipment controls and how to do simple operations, such as changing the projector lamp.

- Make sure that basic spare parts are available.

- Quickly preview your slides and videos before the audience starts arriving at the venue.

- Don't push any buttons whose functions you don't know on the video/projection equipment. Check the manual or talk to the right people.

- During your preview, walk around the presentation room and make sure everybody in the audience can see the picture clearly and hear the sound.

- To show clips from the same video, know exactly where to stop, where to fast forward, etc., and cue up each segment in advance, so your

audience does not have to wait as you struggle to
start at the right location.

- If you want to show clips from multiple video
cassettes, you may "cut and paste" them onto
one cassette for the sake of convenience.
(Caution: Copyright laws may apply.)

4. **Make your media work for you.** Chapter 13 provides
specific tips on LCD and OHP slides, whereas ideas
on effective use of flip charts are listed below.

- Write only on the top two-thirds of the paper.

- Use different colored markers.

- Prepare all or part of your charts in advance, if
appropriate.

- Pencil in notes to yourself on the chart to remind
you as you build your points.

- Tear, in advance, the perforation at the top of
each chart three inches on either side to make it
easier to tear off and post.

- Post charts on the wall as necessary. Have cut
pieces of tape ready for posting or use Post-it®
brand charts with glue.

- It may be necessary to use more than one flip-
chart stand, especially when brainstorming.
Have each "recorder" record every *other*
comment.

12. EQUIPMENT ETIQUETTE

1. **Be sensitive to the audience.** When using AV equipment, make sure the audience is not distracted by or annoyed with the equipment or the way you handle it. Minimize the time you spend in front of the audience preparing/fixing the equipment.

2. **Do not block the view.** Stay clear of audience's line of sight with the TV and the projection screens.

3. **Avoid distractions.** Audience members may be distracted by or irritated with idly sitting equipment and improper handling of the equipment. Here are some tips to minimize such feelings:

    -   Do not leave the OHP light on with a blank white spot glaring on the screen. Turning off the projector eliminates the fan noise and also extends the lamp life.

- Similarly, spare the audience from the screensaver on your laptop projected on the screen during the idle time.

- Avoid displaying any slide (OHP or LCD) for too long on the screen once you have moved on to a different topic or even if you are on the same topic but in an elaborate discussion. You may turn off the OHP or "mute" the LCD projector.

- Do not leave the TV on with a blank blue screen or, even worse, a "snow screen."

- Make sure that the TV volume is not at an unbearable level when you turn it on for the audience.

4. **Do not waste time.** If you cannot fix any equipment problems within a minute, do not test your audience's patience or waste their time. Be prepared for such incidents and quickly move on with minimal disruption to the continuity of your presentation. If you are in dire need of the equipment, you may call for an impromptu break.

5. **Stay calm.** When equipment problems occur, do not lose your composure. Do not curse at the equipment or blame your host or the facility

operators. Appropriate humor may serve you well in these types of situations.

6. **Be organized.** Have your LCD slides and the video cued up and ready to go when you need them. With the former, have all the slides in one file, if possible, to avoid going through file opening procedures while the audience is waiting. With the video player, make sure the color and the sound levels are adjusted in advance.

7. **Dim the lights only if necessary.** Dark rooms are not conducive to learning. Avoid dimming the room lights as much as possible. Prepare two sets of slides, one with dark color letters on a light background and the other vice versa. (See Chapter 13.) Use the set that doesn't require dimmed lighting. Try to avoid showing videos or slides that require dimmed light right after lunch.

8. **Master microphone matters.** You probably do not need a microphone for an audience with less than 30 members. When you use one, you may follow these guidelines:

    *   Irrespective of the type of mike you use, with advance preparation, make sure you have the volume control set at the right level.

- If you are speaking from behind a lectern with an attached mike, make sure it is at the right length. Do not lean forward to speak into the mike.

- If you intend to move freely on the stage in front of the audience or among the seats, use a cordless mike. If you want to use both your hands freely for more animated gestures, a lavaliere mike is preferable.

- With lavaliere mikes, make sure you turn them on right before you start to speak and turn them off immediately after you finish. It is not uncommon for speakers to go to the bathrooms with the mikes on, creating some potentially embarrassing situations.

- Keep spare batteries available for lavaliere mikes.

13. SLIDE RULES

1. **Use slides only if necessary.** For short speeches (1 to 2 hours), avoid them all together unless you have a compelling reason to use them. The only reason you would want to use slides is to show pictures, images, or charts with numeric data (which actually can be provided to the audience in the form of a handout). For training sessions, they also serve well for highlighting key points. Use slides only to supplement your presentation. A common bad practice for many speakers and trainers is to go through a series of slides and supplement *them* with discussion.

2. **Don't read from the screen.** At all costs, avoid reading from any medium, such as a screen, laptop, manual, text book, note paper, etc.

3. **Follow the 7x7 rule.** Excluding the title, limit the text on the slide to seven lines per slide and seven words per line. This rule applies even to charts of numerical data with several rows and columns.

Present only the summary information, and if necessary, provide a handout for details.

4. **Prepare two sets.** Prepare two sets of your slides, one with dark color text on a light color background and the other vice versa. Try both in your presentation room and pick the set that works better for the light conditions in the room. Avoid dimming the lights as much as you can. The most effective colors are yellow and white text on a dark blue background; black and dark blue text on a light yellow background.

5. **Use at least 32-point font for text.** Not everybody has 20/20 vision. Even with perfect vision, people sitting in the back of the presentation room may not be able to see the text on the screen with smaller font.

6. **Steer clear of sound effects.** Sounds are distracting. Do not use sound with your slides unless it adds value.

7. **Shy away from excessive animation.** With the power of software, you can create jazzy slides and show off your slide-making skills, but unless you are speaking about how to make slides, your true message will be lost in the fancy animation.

8. **Reveal points progressively.** Wherever it makes sense, reveal points on the slides one after the other. When using OHP, you may place "revealing" paper *under* the slide and reveal each point at a time.

9. **Use a laser pointer.** Laser pointers have become very inexpensive and are widely available today. To highlight with a pointer, aim at the target area on the slide, click once, and release the light button immediately. Holding the button and moving the red light across the screen is distracting and annoying to the audience. For OHP, you may also place a pointer on the slide itself on top of the glass. Do not use your hands to point, especially if it means turning your back to the audience.

10. **Do not talk to the screen.** Also, avoid talking to your laptop. Always face the audience.

11. **Have backups.** Always carry a disk containing your presentation slides just in case any problems arise with your file on the hard drive of your laptop. Also, keep the same file as another backup on your email server. All of us—including Bill Gates, chairman of Microsoft—have experienced computer crashes at the most unwanted times. (Gates's laptop crashed exactly when he was introducing Windows 95 to the world at

Microsoft's new product launch show.) Use OHP as your backup to LCD. If OHP fails, take advantage of flip charts. If every AV aid fails, ultimately you must be prepared to conduct your session without any aids and especially without reading from your notes. The show must go on!

14. BANISHING BUTTERFLIES

1. **Admit you have stage fright.** Aram Bakshian, Jr., a speechwriter of President Ronald Reagan, believes: "As with alcoholism, there's no known cure for stage fright. You're either a 'chronic' sufferer or a 'recovering' sufferer." In either case, you can minimize that suffering. Or you can even take advantage of it by first acknowledging it and then turning it into positive tension.

2. **Create a compelling mental focus.** Banishing anxiety in a presentation and appearing cool and confident is an internal game. The body will feel what the brain tells it to feel. When you tell yourself you hate giving presentations or entertain thoughts of failure, you are likely to create just the outcomes you don't want. Train your brain to focus on the positive reasons you were asked to speak and the benefits you will receive from the talk.

3.   **Program a "positive picture" into your brain.**
Visualize a successful outcome with the audience.
Picture yourself, if you can, in the exact room in
which you will be presenting. See the audience rise
in thunderous applause when you have finished!
You may not actually get a standing ovation, but
you will be reminding your brain that you are a
great speaker and deserve the applause.

4.   **Prepare, prepare, and prepare.** Prepare well in
advance and become confident about not only the
subject matter, but also the delivery of the
presentation itself. Hasty or poor preparation leads
to less confidence, which creates anxiety.

5.   **Rehearse the opening repeatedly.** Practice your
whole presentation a few times, but rehearse the
first five minutes at least fifteen times. Know your
opening backward and forward, and in your sleep.
While memorizing your presentation is not a good
idea, memorizing the first three lines is highly
recommended. If you can get through the first three
minutes, your heart rate will decrease and you will
settle down into the presentation.

6.   **Practice your presentation out loud.** Standing up,
preferably in the room you will be speaking in and
in the clothes—especially the shoes—that you will

be wearing, practice out loud the entire presentation. This is helpful if it is relatively short, as in a keynote speech. For longer presentations, such as seminars and training sessions, you may practice the openings, closings, and key portions of your program. This will help you alleviate some of the anxiety of the unknown.

7.   **Nix negativity about the audience.** Have you ever been in the audience when the speaker was nervous? Didn't you feel empathy for the person and want her to calm down and succeed? Most audiences are rooting for the speaker. Do not make yourself go mad thinking that the audience wants to tear you apart. Even if you are defending your Ph.D. dissertation, although they may ask tough questions, your professor and committee sincerely want you to pass.

8.   **Remember to breathe!** Right before a presentation, your heart rate will often rise from an average of 90 beats a minute to 110 or 120. Take deep cleansing breaths to control the heart rate and keep calm. Once you start, the heart rate may hit 140! That's like doing aerobics! Now more than ever it is important to take deep diaphragmatic breaths. Slow down a bit and pause between sentences to breathe. After the first five minutes, your heart rate will

subside to a reasonable level and you will feel comfortable.

9.   **Get to know the audience.** Meet, greet, and socialize with your audience as they come into the presentation room and settle in. This will help you take your mind off your presentation and help you reduce the anxiety. Plus, you can start establishing rapport with your customers.

10. **"Get centered."** Just prior to starting your presentation, take several deep breaths—in through the nose and out through the mouth. Sip some water. (Avoid ice water because it irritates the throat. Do not drink carbonated beverages because they create gas.) Walk to the podium confidently. Stand erect with straight posture. Look at the audience, smile, and begin with a bang.

11. **Gain strength from affirmations.** Make 3x5-inch affirmation cards saying things like, "I am articulate," "I am confident," or "I am funny." Read them to yourself a few times the night before and the day of the presentation. Okay, it reeks of a *Saturday Night Live* skit, but don't roll your eyes! This technique really works. Try it! See for yourself!

12. **Pick out "friendly faces."** Before you begin your talk, look around the room and choose some

friendly faces, those who will send you a smile or other positive energy. (If you follow Tip No. 8 above, you already should know who they are!) Focus on these "friends" when you start, especially if you get nervous. Then slowly look around for new "friends" and expand your eye contact.

13.   **Keep your hands free.** Before you talk, empty your pockets. Keep your hands free of paper, pencils, pens, pointers, or any distracting objects you might be apt to play with or that may become a distraction to the audience. Do not constantly fix your clothes, push up your glasses when they are not slipping, or touch your face or hair. These are signs of self-consciousness and nervousness that will not translate well to the audience.

14.   **No alterations prior to show time!** Never alter your presentation within 24 hours from its delivery time. If you are a semi-experienced speaker, you may cut that time down to four hours. Unless you are a seasoned pro, last minute changes will only cause you to fear that something will go wrong because you have not rehearsed it enough.

15.   **Do not memorize.** Never memorize your presentation word for word, especially if you are nervous. If you do, you may forget one tiny piece—which is very likely—and throw yourself into a

panic. Use bulleted notes or a script to stay on track.

16. **Never ever visualize or verbalize negative outcomes**. The brain is like a computer—garbage in, garbage out. If you imagine the audience not laughing at a joke you tell, you can pretty much be sure this will happen. Even if it doesn't happen, it will make you miserable and fearful of being yourself, and that will cause you to spend your energy battling your fear instead of connecting with the audience.

17. **Show up early.** Woody Allen famously said: "85% of success is showing up." For 100% success, show up early. Or even better, arrive at the venue the day before to make sure the room layout, equipment, and other logistics are taken care of. This will mean fewer things that could cause anxiety.

15. HANDLING DIFFICULT PEOPLE

1. **Always show respect.** Challenging individuals—there are different types as we will discuss below—need to be skillfully handled. Always show respect for the individual and protect his or her esteem, and you will gain the audience's support. You have the power to embarrass difficult people in your role as a speaker or trainer, but you should rarely use it. The audience may even resent a difficult individual for a long while, yet if you display any negative intent, such as anger or punishment, they are likely to shift loyalties. Below are tips for handling different types of difficult people. Although these may be more applicable to training situations, they have merit even with short speeches.

2. **"Know it alls" and "show-offs."** A know-it-all is a person who thinks he is (or truly is) an expert in the subject matter and wants to "show off." If he is frequently asking questions on material that you will shortly be covering, just say, *"Please hold off on*

that question. We will cover that topic shortly in a later section." If he is trying to answer every question you are posing to your entire audience group, you may say, *"Let's hear from someone new."* Or *"Justin, I suspect you know the answer, but let's see who else has an idea."* Another effective approach is taking such people aside at the break and saying, *"Mary, I am impressed with your level of knowledge on the subject. The class is letting you carry all the weight in the discussions. I would like to ask you to hang back this module and let them carry the ball. If I need you to bail me out, I will let you know."* Always keep your tone pleasant.

3.   **"Hyper inquisitives."** These people ask too many questions and may dominate the discussion. You may ask such people to make a list and tell them that you will give them some one-on-one time during the break.

4.   **"Wind bags."** These are people who go into elaborate monologues without making any significant points or asking questions. Find a spot when they pause and jump in to say, *"Good point, if I may summarize what Paul said …,"* and then summarize quickly for them and move on. Or, as appropriate, ask the individual what his specific question is.

5.   **Hecklers.** A heckler is usually resentful and will exhibit challenges with a slightly (or not so slightly) vindictive tone. *Never* argue or show any anger with a person like this. Just have a light comeback and move on. You may slowly amble toward the heckler with a smile and say sweetly, *"There's one in every crowd, you know, and I think I found out who it is today."* The audience is waiting for you to break the tension when this person acts out. Some humor will help and maybe even turn the person around. Never let a heckler have the last word, but always keep it light.

6.   **"Yeah, but…" complainers.** Some people are never happy with any of your ideas or solutions. They might repeatedly challenge you by bringing up very specific scenarios and asking for advice. Here are some tips on what you might say: *"There is no magic bullet, but what you might do is.…"* Or *"Your situation definitely is different and unique. Based on what we have discussed, do* you *have any ideas?"* Or *"You seem to have very specific challenging situations. Maybe we can discuss these one-on-one at the end of this session without taking up everybody's time."* Again, keep your tone pleasant.

7.   **Avoid arguments.** Often complainers are simply venting. They are problem-centered rather than

solution-centered. Get them to focus on solutions. If they keep turning down every solution (yeah, but…), ask them to tell you what they have tried that *does* work. Use a facilitative (questioning) approach rather than a statement-centered approach.

8. **Let them "dump their bucket."** If you know in advance that you are going to face a resentful group (no fault of yours), it is a good idea to let them vocalize their issues or complaints at the beginning of your session as an icebreaker. You may ask, *"What are the challenges or issues you are facing right now concerning …?"* Write these on a visual for a few minutes, and then turn the focus to solutions.

9. **"Precall" problems.** If you already know about existing problems or negative issues that your audience is going to challenge you on, you may bring them up yourself. For example, in a highly bureaucratic organization, your audience may seem victimized and have a helpless mentality that wants to blame management for all of its problems. Admit that things aren't perfect, but explain that spending energy on that won't help. Make it clear that you will be focusing on the solutions and you need their help.

10. **Never lose your temper.** Always keep cool and calm in handling difficult people. Be in control. Don't let the situation get out of hand.

"We are what we repeatedly do."

—*Aristotle*

16. HAVE ANY QUESTIONS?

1. **Encourage questions.** Whether it is a short speech or a long training session, first let your audience know that you will take questions. Make it clear as to when you will take questions. For short speeches, the best time is at the end, whereas in seminars, courses, workshops, etc., questions should be taken any time, unless specific circumstances call for the contrary.

2. **Pause for questions.** In training sessions, stop frequently and ask if there are any questions before you move on.

3. **Avoid pointing fingers.** When taking questions, avoid pointing your finger at the questioner. Use an open palm to acknowledge or call upon people.

4. **Acknowledge questions positively.** Everyone has a right to ask questions and make comments, even if it does not fit with your agenda or what you think

about the topic. Start your response by saying, *"It's a great (good, interesting, etc.) question."* Use different phrases each time.

5. **Understand the question.** Sometimes in addition to understanding the question itself, you may want to probe into the intent of the question by asking counter-questions yourself. This gives you more insight into where the questioner is coming from and helps you answer it more effectively. Also, listen to the tone of the question. Is it really a set-up? Does the questioner seem to have any hidden agenda?

6. **Repeat the question.** Irrespective of the size of the audience, it is always a good idea to repeat the question in your own words for the entire audience. Then you may ask the questioner whether you got the question right, which ensures understanding on your part. Furthermore, it helps the rest of the audience understand as well.

7. **Use proper audio equipment.** For a large audience, make sure in advance that there are standing microphones or "runners" with microphones available.

8. **Make eye contact.** When you answer a question, begin by making eye contact with the questioner, and then include everyone else.

9.   **Be concise.** Provide simple, specific, direct answers. Avoid long elaborate discussions. Sometimes you may give a quick, direct answer first and then discuss your point. With long drawn-out answers, people may lose track of the original question and think that you did not understand and/or answer the question properly.

10.   **Ensure questioner satisfaction.** After responding to the question, make sure the questioner is satisfied. You may ask, *"Did I answer your question?"* or *"Does that help?"* If the answer seems unsatisfactory, ask them if they have a follow-up question and try to elaborate more on your answer. If you are not getting anywhere, you may tell the questioner to see you after the session for a one-on-one discussion.

11.   **Avoid dialogues.** Do not get ensnared into a dialogue with one person.

12.   **Do not turn a statement into a question.** Sometimes the questioner really wants to make a statement. Listen to the tone. If it seems like he or she already knows the answer, simply reflect it back: *"What do* you *think?"*

13.   **Accept ignorance.** Don't be afraid to say *"I don't know"* if you don't know the answer. You may ask

the audience if anybody has an answer, or you may offer to get back to the questioner with an answer at a later time. If you have any resources that may provide the answer, furnish that information or point questioners in the right direction to get their own answers.

14. **Table irrelevant questions.** If the question seems irrelevant, point out that you believe it is outside the scope of the topic at hand. You can either drop the issue there or ask the audience if they have any interest in the question. If the majority expresses interest, you may either address the question at that time or, if time permits, at a later point in the presentation.

17. FEEDBACK LOOPS

1.   **Get feedback.** Have both formal and informal evaluations of your presentations. Take advantage of the feedback to continuously improve and become "best in class" speaker or trainer.

2.   **Use formal evaluations.** For every talk or training session, make sure to provide and receive structured, written evaluations from your audience. Ask for feedback at least in four broad areas: physical environment, content, training materials, and speaker/trainer performance.

3.   **Review the evaluation form in advance.** Make sure you address the items in that form during your presentation.

4.   **Ask for DIGs and DIBs:** DIG stands for "Did It Good" and DIB for "Do It Better." Casually ask your host/sponsor and the audience for things that you did well and things you can do better. This

approach is very constructive with focus on the positives and future improvements.

5.   **Conduct midcourse evaluations.** In long training programs, conduct informal evaluations (for example, DIGs/DIBs) once or twice during the training to make necessary midcourse corrections and minimize surprises at the end.

6.   **Explain evaluation forms.** Ask your host to (or you yourself can) remind the participants about the evaluation forms and mention that their feedback is important. Ask them to write down specific comments in addition to providing a numeric rating. These comments will be extremely valuable for improving your presentation skills.

7,   **Seek feedback from mentors and experts.** Ask your colleagues (speakers/trainers) to attend your presentation and give you objective feedback. Again, you can ask for DIGs and DIBs. You can gain tremendous insight into what you are doing well and how you can improve through feedback from these experts.

8.   **Improve continuously.** Look for general trends in the feedback. Always focus on frequently made comments. There is no reason to get too excited on

one isolated outstanding positive comment or, more important, to get depressed about one negative outlier. Such comments are truly unworthy of your time. Continue to do the things that your customers are giving you good marks on and incessantly make adjustments, where necessary, to improve and excel.

"The man who does not read good books has no advantage over the man who can't read them."

—*Mark Twain*

18. TEN AUDIENCE TURNOFFS

1. **Starting with an apology.** Never start your presentation in a negative way, as it sets a "downer" tone that will likely carry over to the meat of your talk. Begin with your usual "bang," and if the situation warrants an apology, make mention of it after you have set the tone and established your personal power.

2. **"Off color" humor.** If humor is your style, keep it up, but be careful how you use it. You don't want to risk offending or insulting anyone or distracting them from your key points. First, be sure your humor is relevant to the topic at hand: Does it make your point? Steer clear of ridicule, intimidation, and off-color humor related to sex, race, nationality, etc. Very few speakers can pull off this "Don Rickles" type humor.

3. **The "I am awesome" syndrome.** Avoid being condescending, or treating the audience like they

are "broken" and that you, the "mighty one," is here to enlighten the common people. Audiences do not tune in to someone who does not respect them and genuinely want to help them.

4.   **Coming off "canned."** Being polished is important, but not at the expense of being real. Audiences see right through that and will think you have given the talk too many times. Presenters who are mechanical with seamless delivery often seem fake. Use natural body language and your own conversational style to establish your personal credibility, and build rapport by engaging the audience and tailoring your talk to them.

5.   **Reading.** Boring. Enough said.

6.   **Breaking time agreements.** Be aware of your allocated speaking time and stick to it like you are keeping your word. Starting late or going over time will have participants checking their watches instead of listening to you. Make your speeches shorter, not longer. Have you heard of anybody complaining about a speech being too short or finishing too early? President Franklin D. Roosevelt's advice to his son on speechmaking was: "Be sincere, be brief, be seated."

7.   **Excessive personal stories.** This one often goes along with the "I am awesome" syndrome. Avoid

talking too much about yourself and never bring your personal problems to the podium. Above all, never, ever, tell someone else's story as if it happened to you when it didn't. Use stories about a variety of people and subjects, give credit when credit is due, and better yet, tell the stories of the people in your audience. Keep the names anonymous as appropriate.

8. **Overused stories.** Nothing makes an audience roll their eyes more than a story that's been told too many times. Know your audience. If you speak before the same group twice, avoid using the same examples or anecdotes. Change your stories regularly for each audience. Take the time to find fresh, novel, and original anecdotes.

9. **Distracting appearance or mannerisms**. You want the audience to focus on your message not your wild tie, excessive jewelry, jingling pocket change, repetitive gestures, or other distractions.

10. **Disorganization.** Examples of disorganization include muddled information flow, and rummaging for pens, pointers, transparencies, handouts, etc. These can annoy the audience and make you look unprepared. Do the planning. Get to the presentation room early and see that the space is set up properly to meet your needs.

"Great is the art of beginning; greater is the art of finishing."

—*Henry Wadsworth Longfellow*

19. FORCEFUL FINALES

1. **End with a bang.** Close your presentation not just by summarizing key points. Make it different, unique, and **bold**.

2. **Tie your opening and closing together.** This will help you weave a common thread throughout the presentation so you can tie it up into a complete package at the end.

3. **Nail the ending.** Have a final statement prepared and even memorize it. You want to make it exactly the way you want it without any slip-ups whatsoever. Make that statement simple and succinct, yet powerful. If you expect an applause, you may end your statement with some kind of a physical salutation, something that acts as a cue for the audience. Margaret Thatcher, former British prime minister, usually makes her final statement, clears her throat as she looks down, and steps back with a powerful voice and says, "Thank you."

4.   **Tell an inspirational story.** Often a story that tells of one who overcame obstacles or persisted to a final win will give your group confidence to make a change, make a difference, or take some action you wish them to take.

5.   **End with a challenge.** This is especially effective with competitive people or with a group that has a tremendous task ahead.

6.   **Ask the audience to vocalize their goals.** This approach works best with training classes. You may ask the participants to write down or vocally express goals based on what they have just learned. Encourage them to start using their newfound knowledge within 72 hours for the best return on their investment.

7.   **Have the audience complete a final project.** Again, this works well with training classes. Have audience members apply all the information they have learned in the class toward a final project. This has enormous practical value and gives them a sense of closure.

8.   **Create a visual collage put to music.** This works very effectively for company meetings that last several days, professional conferences, or

conventions. Use a video or slides of images of the days the group spent together. Pick appropriate music to combine with the images to create a complete package of visual, audio, and emotional stimulation that will send your customers away on a high note.

9. **Don't drag the finish line.** Don't speak on for more than a couple of minutes after you say, "In conclusion …" or "Finally.…" Such phrases give the audience a clear signal that the talk is almost over. Going on and on at this point can damage the positive gains you may have made so far and take away the impact of not just the closing, but the entire presentation.

10. **Thank the audience personally.** When you have ended your talk, break eye contact and make your way to the door to shake participants' hands as they leave.

11. **Don't run out immediately after the speech.** Take time to thank the sponsor or contact for the event personally. Ask him or her for informal feedback. Stick around for a while for interested audience members to stop by and say goodbye.

"Human history in essence is a history of ideas."

—*H. G. Wells*

20. BONUS BITES

1. Join professional associations, such as Toastmasters International, American Society of Training and Development, and the National Speakers' Association.

2. Subscribe to training journals, such as *Training* (Lakewood Publications) and *Training and Development* (American Society of Training and Development).

3. Read at least 10 percent outside your area of expertise and improve your general knowledge.

4. Always try new speaking and training techniques and keep fine-tuning the old.

5. Constantly look for new stories, jokes, or statistics. Keep a journal to record these.

6.   Stay up to date on the newest studies and materials in your subject area(s).

7.   Watch other speakers and trainers in action and learn from their triumphs and mistakes. Always take notes for future use.

8.   Develop a group of superior speakers with whom to share information and success/failure stories.

9.   Audio/videotape your presentations, assess them, and improve your style continuously.

10. Always keep your energy, enthusiasm, and passion high.

ABOUT THE AUTHORS

Dr. Prasad Kodukula (President, Kodukula & Associates, Inc.) is a motivational speaker, accomplished engineer, award-winning educator, executive coach, and inventor with twenty years of professional experience. He regularly speaks on a variety of topics including communication skills, leadership, project management, change management, and creativity/innovation. Known for his boundless energy and enthusiasm, Prasad consistently receives rave reviews on his keynote speeches and seminars from audiences spanning twelve countries. His clients include fifteen of the Fortune 100 companies and the United States Government. He is a contributing author on four books and has co-authored two books and more than forty technical articles.

Ms. Susan Meyer-Miller (President, SpeakerUSA) is a motivational speaker, business trainer, and management consultant specializing in communication skills, leadership, customer service, and women's issues. She has spoken to people in eight countries and is consistently praised for her dynamism and humor. She has trained professionals in the private and public sectors and non-profit organizations. Susan is an active writer and has won regional and national awards with the American Business Women's Association, where she has held many leadership positions. She is the author of the book *SOS! 101 Solutions to Overcome Stress*.

LaVergne, TN USA
08 July 2010
188702LV00001B/13/A